Y0-CBA-587

Four Marks
of a
Total Christian

Bruce Shelley

While this book is designed for the reader's personal enjoyment and profit, it is also intended for group study. A leader's guide is available from your local bookstore or from the publisher at 75¢.

VICTOR BOOKS

a division of SP Publications, Inc., Wheaton, Illinois

Offices also in Fullerton, California • Whitby, Ontario, Canada • London, England

Unless otherwise noted, Scripture quotations are from
The *New International Version: New Testament* (NIV),
© 1973, The New York Bible Society. Other quotations
are from the *New American Standard Bible* (NASB), ©
1960, 1962, 1963, 1968, 1971, 1972, 1973. The Lock-
man Foundation, La Habra, California, and the King
James Version (KJV). All quotations used by permission.

Library of Congress Catalog Number:
ISBN: 0-88207-512-8

© 1978 by SP Publications, Inc. World rights reserved
Printed in the United States of America

VICTOR BOOKS
A division of SP Publications, Inc.
P.O. Box 1825 • Wheaton, Ill. 60187

Contents

1

Jesus Christ:

The Crux of
the Matter

In his story *The Country of the Blind,* H. G. Wells tells how a traveler came to a strange valley, cut off from the rest of the world by precipitous walls, in which all the people were blind. He lived for a while in this strange place but was considered strange by the natives. Their experts said, "His brain is affected by these queer things called the eyes which keep it in a constant state of irritation and distraction." And they concluded that he would never be normal until his eyes were removed!

The traveler fell in love with a sightless girl who pleaded with him to have his eyes removed so that he and she might live together in happiness. But one morning he saw the sun rise behind the rocks and the meadows beautiful with white flowers. No longer could he be content in the valley of darkness. He climbed back to the land where men walk in the light.

Jesus the Light

The story illustrates the problem Jesus faced in this sin-infected world. The Apostle John put it this way: "Light has come into the world, but men loved darkness instead of light because their deeds were evil. Everyone who does evil hates the light, and will not come into the light for fear that his deeds will be exposed. But whoever lives by the truth comes into the light" (John 3:19-21). The Gospels are filled with accounts of Jesus' attempts to open the eyes of people who would not see the truth. He is still at it, with us. In a world of darkness, what does it mean to come to the light? What does it mean to be a follower of Christ in a world of blind men? What is Christianity?

The questions are simple enough, but ask almost any group of people "What does it mean to be a Christian?" and you will get an assortment of answers. In our evangelical view of Christianity, we tend to stress one side of the truth to the exclusion of another. Some Christians think that the true faith is an accurate credal statement. Others contend that it is some high voltage religious experience. Others insist that it is the influence for good in the world. Still others argue that it is membership in a particular church.

Creed, conversion, conduct, church—there is an element of truth in each of these answers. The problem lies in seeing the whole picture. An anonymous songwriter voiced our need in verse:

If we could see,
If we could know,
We often say,

But God in love
    A veil doth throw
Across our way;

    We cannot see
What lies before,
    And so we cling
To Him the more,

    He leads us till
This life is o'er
    Trust and obey.

The imagery of the Book of the Revelation provides a glimpse of what it means to be a total Christian. In the culminating vision God gave to John, the city "prepared as a bride . . . for her husband" (Rev. 21:2) probably represents the glorified people of God. John repeats the words he heard, "God Himself will be with them and be their God" (21:3).

The Apostle notes that there is no temple in this city—unusual for any ancient town—but there is no need for a temple here. Nor do the sun and moon shine on the city, "because the Lord God Almighty and the Lamb" are the temple and the city's light and life (21:22-23).

John is apparently making the point that God's people are called His people because God the Almighty and Jesus the Lamb are in their midst. The vision reveals the heart of Christian reality: seeing life, relationships, and ministry as God sees them.

The Apostle John also describes the Holy City as "laid out like a square" from which are excluded "the cowardly, the unbelieving, the vile, the murderers, the sexually immoral, those who practice magic arts, the idolators and all liars" (Rev. 21:8, 16). Like the city "foursquare," total Christianity has four distinctive but inseparably related sides: obedience, truth, experience, and community. We will examine each of these later.

Jesus, Central to Our Faith

Most people grasp truths more readily when conversing with someone who knows what he is talking about. The Gospels give us a chance to do this because they contain a number of conversations Jesus had with people.

In an intimate conversation Jesus had with His closest followers—as recorded in John 13 and 14—we find again the idea that "the Lamb of God" in our midst is the heart of Christian reality, the light by which we see life as God sees it. In that sense this passage is an introduction to others dealing with the dimensions of total Christianity. It is a rewarding study, however, because as we struggle and grope through the shadows of our times, there is some comfort in knowing that the first disciples stumbled through theirs.

John recorded the conversations this way:

When [Judas] was gone, Jesus said, "Now is the Son of Man glorified and God is glorified in Him. If God is glorified in Him, then God will glorify the Son in Himself, and will glorify Him at once.

"My children, I will be with you only a little longer. You will look for Me, and just as I told the Jews, so I tell you now: Where I am going, you cannot come. . . ."

Simon Peter asked Him, "Lord, where are You going?"

Jesus replied, "Where I am going, you cannot follow now, but you will follow later."

Peter asked, "Lord, why can't I follow You now? I will lay down my life for You."

Then Jesus answered, "Will you really lay down your life for Me? I tell you the truth, before the rooster crows, you will disown Me three times!

"Do not let your hearts be troubled. Trust in God; trust also in Me. There are many rooms in My Father's house; otherwise, I would have told you. I am going there to prepare a place for you. And if I go and prepare a place for you, I will come back and take you to be with Me that you also may be where I am. You know the way to the place where I am going."

Thomas said to Him, "Lord, we don't know where You are going, so how can we know the way?"

Jesus answered, "I am the way—and the truth and the life. No one comes to the Father except through Me. If you really knew Me, you would know My Father as well. From now on, you do know Him and have seen Him."

Philip said, "Lord, show us the Father and that will be enough for us."

Jesus answered, "Don't you know Me, Philip, even after I have been among you for such a long time? Anyone who has seen Me has seen the Father. How can you say, 'Show us the Father'? Don't you believe that I am in the Father, and that the Father is in Me? The words I say to you are not just My own. Rather, it is the Father, living in Me, who is doing His work. . . ."

Then Judas (not Judas Iscariot) said, "But, Lord, why do You intend to show Yourself to us and not to the world?"

Jesus replied, "If anyone loves Me, he will obey My teaching. My Father will love him, and We will come to him and make our home with him. He who does not love Me will not obey My teaching. These words you hear are not My own; they belong to the Father who sent Me. All this I have spoken while still with you" (John 13:31-33, 36—14:10, 22-25).

After three years, on the eve of His death, Jesus found His closest friends unable to see clearly the central reality of discipleship. In this conversation with them on the way to the garden for prayer, each revealed his inability to see what faith in Jesus meant.

Faith in Jesus and Obedience

Peter, the activist, spoke first (John 13:36-37). When Jesus announced His impending departure, Peter asked at once, "Lord, where are You going?" Jesus responded that none of them could follow Him just yet. But Peter wouldn't have any of this.

"Why can't I follow You now?" he asked. "I will lay down my life for You" (v. 37).

Peter had caught a glimpse of "the city" at the time Jesus was transfigured (Matt. 17:1-8). He knew that Jesus was the "Light of the world" (John 8:12). He had declared, "You [Jesus] are the Christ, the Son of the living God (Matt. 16:16).

Yet so much of his blindness remained. He could not control his impetuosity. He still thought that obedience to Christ meant the heroic deed, the great sacrifice. "I'll lay down my life for You."

Surely Peter was the first "American" Christian. He, like so many of us, had to be doing something for the Lord. If Christian service is the thing, then let's do it up in style. "Here is my glossy photo! Have you seen my slides from the bush?"

The appearance of dedication and sacrifice must be among the greatest temptations for "full-time" servants of Christ! So many people consider them extraordinary saints! Yet the human heart never lacks for ways to make us hollow men and women. Among the most subtle is the appearance of sacrificial service.

But don't misunderstand. The Lord doesn't deny the intrusion of the Cross—for Himself or for Peter. In biblical Christianity there is no salvation without suffering. A disciple is not above his master!

What Jesus challenges is not Peter's zeal, but his confidence. "Will you really lay down your life for Me? I tell you the truth, before the rooster crows, you will disown Me three times!" (John 13:38)

Peter's trouble was that he had come to think of

his dedication as sacrifice. He had come to see the ministry in terms of hardship. And that is always a dangerous view for a servant of God.

When we begin to think that we are laying down our lives for the Lord, we are only a step away from calling for the spotlights. . . .

Where is the praise I deserve?

I don't mind dying, but could you increase my salary in the interim?

If I am to give my life in this hot and mosquito-infested country, please see that some Christian magazine gets the story. . . .

Obeying Jesus, Peter had to learn, is never mere obedience. It is trust in overalls.

"Peter," said Jesus, "don't let your heart be agitated. You are at cross-purposes with yourself.

"You trust in God, now trust in *Me*." As the hymn-writer George Duffield wrote,

The arm of flesh
will fail you;
Ye dare not
trust your own.

Faith in Jesus and Truth

Thomas, the skeptic, responded to Jesus' statements about His going away. When Jesus mentioned leaving to prepare a place, he said bluntly, "Lord, we don't know where You are going, so how can we know the way?" (John 14:5)

You find no call for dedication here. The tone is resignation. You can't act on what you don't know.

Stop the action!

Suspend all judgment!

Drop out!

Of all the disciples, Thomas is the best candidate for the counter-culture. He sees through Peter's idealism. In his gloom his attitude is "Why sweat it?" Thomas hasn't found life's purpose, so why get involved?

It is possible to hide behind the quest for truth. We can find comfort in saying, "We don't have all the answers, so why commit ourselves?"

Do we ever do that? Have we stopped taking risks for God because we have found a kind of comfort in the familiar? And then do we cover our complacency by saying, "How do we know it will work out?" or "We've never done it that way before"?

It is possible to make a religion of reserving judgment. We spend our time checking on the escape hatches. We can treat God and the ministry like the bridegroom at the altar who when asked, "Do you take this woman to be your lawfully wedded wife?" answered, "That all depends."

Despite his doubts, there is something admirable in Questioning Thomas. Gullibility is a mark of our age and God doesn't ask us to check our brains at the door of the church.

But we cannot postpone forever what we are going to do about eternal matters. Doubt is acceptable as a foyer to faith. We never really believe until we have questioned. But there comes a time when we have to step out of skepticism and into commitment.

That is why Jesus turned Thomas and his quest for truth to Himself.

I am the way—
    the truth and
    the life (John 14:6).

Faith in Jesus and Experience

Philip, the pietist, spoke up at this point. "Lord, show us the Father," he said, "and that will be enough for us" (John 14:8).

Here is the response of a man impatient with beautiful abstractions. He isn't content with God as a sacred Blur. He is dissatisfied with a nameless, impersonal Power in the universe.

"Show us the Father," he says. "God must be real to me—I want Him to manifest Himself in me!"

There are a lot of Philip-like Christians today. They are impatient with orthodoxy's pat answers for their heartfelt hungers. They want to see God at work, to feel His nearness, to know in their hearts that He hasn't forgotten them.

Again there is something right in an experience-orientation. The God of the Bible *is* personal. He yearns and laughs and speaks and hears. And He seeks men to worship Him.

But Philip shows us that there must be a limit to our demands. Our warm heart must never be the object of our search.

Jesus said to Philip, perhaps with a touch of exasperation, "Have I been so long with you and still you do not know Me?

Philip, anyone who has seen Me has seen the Father.

Check My words. Check also My works.

I am in the Father and the Father is in Me."

You see, the only view of God you and I will ever have is found in Jesus Christ. "No man has ever seen God, but God the only Son, who is at the Father's side, has made Him known" (John 1:18).

But do we need any other view of God? Must it be Jesus plus a gift; Jesus plus an experience; Jesus plus a blessing?

But this does not call for an emotionless, grit-your-teeth kind of Christianity. Rather, God takes our memories of Jesus' life and teachings, created by the devout reading of the Bible, and through the Holy Spirit nurtures the life of God in our souls. He reinforces our resolves to please Him. He fosters our willingness to restore broken relationships. He deepens our love for the truth as it is in Jesus.

But something in us dies when, like Philip, we try to establish the terms of the relationship or define the kind of experience.

Jesus said to Philip, "Don't you believe? . . . Believe Me when I say that I am in the Father and the Father is in Me" (John 14:10-11).

Faith in Jesus and Community

Judas—or as he is sometimes called, Thaddaeus—the ecumenist, gives the final response to Jesus (John 14:22). Judas may have felt some unfairness in the ways of God when he asked, "Why do You intend to show Yourself to us and not to the world?" His question is at the heart of liberal theology. What kind of God is the Christian God, if He isn't available or accessible to all men?

Can God be just and limit His revelation

    during a particular time,
    at a particular place,
    to a particular people?

Judas—and every liberal-minded soul since—feels that it is presumptuous of orthodox Christians to insist that God revealed Himself through Jesus alone. What about sincere believers in the Hindu, and Buddhist, and Islamic religions? Do we make too much of Jesus? Are we wrong in saying that no one can claim to be a Christian unless his allegiance is in Jesus Christ?

While doing some independent study at Harvard in 1967, I was reviewing a volume dealing with Phillips Brooks' theology. Brooks, you may recall, was an influential preacher in Boston during the 1880s. In it Brooks said, "Except by Jesus there is no eternal life. Salvation never crosses any threshold where His feet have not been set."

Some reader had underlined "Jesus" and "His" and had written in the margin: "The fatal overestimate of *one individual*. Here is the clash."

I read that note and said to myself: "It is true! Here is the clash. If the line separating those within from those without is to be drawn, let it be drawn here: What do you think of Jesus Christ?"

Why should the line be drawn at Jesus Christ? Notice how He answered Judas: "If anyone"—the Gospel is as broad as the world itself. "If anyone loves *Me*"—it is as narrow as the Cross.

Test Your Vision

You can now test your own spiritual vision of total Christianity.

If, like Peter, you are the activist who wants to do something but are not sure of your directions, Jesus says, *"Trust Me!"*

If, like Thomas, time has made you a skeptic and you no longer expect to find the way, Jesus says, *"Follow Me!"*

If, like Philip, your world is limited to your private experience of God, Jesus says, *"Know Me!"*

And if, like Judas, you are seeking to identify a Christian by human standards, Jesus says, *"Love Me!"*

Herbert Butterfield, the late Professor of Modern History at Cambridge, said this about what should be one's attitude toward Christ:

I have nothing to say at the finish except that if one wants a permanent rock in life and goes deep enough for it, it is difficult for historical events to shake it. There are times when we can never meet the future with sufficient elasticity of mind, especially if we are locked in the contemporary systems of thought. We can do worse than remember a principle which both gives us a firm Rock and leaves us the maximum elasticity for our minds: the principle: Hold to Christ, and for the rest be totally uncommitted (*Christianity and History*, G. Bell, 1954, pp. 145-146).

That, I think, is the starting point for a grasp of Total Christianity.

2

Obedience:

The Mark of
Christian Conduct

A *Peanuts* cartoon shows Charlie Brown filling two puppy bowls with food.

"Suppertime!" he yells.

Snoopy comes up and Charlie says, "I'm going to be gone all day tomorrow, so I've brought you an extra supper. I'd advise you not to be greedy and eat it before tomorrow."

Snoopy eats one bowl of food and then stretches out on the roof of his doghouse. He begins to think of the other bowl and this brings on a case of delirium tremens. He breaks out in a sweat. He struggles with himself and finally lunges at the second bowl and devours the food!

Back on top of his house he says, "I'm glad I ate it . . . I would have hated myself if tomorrow never came."

What a picture of our indulgent age! Of a pregnant 18-year-old, frantically calling for a minister to do a rush job on her wedding; of a 17-year-old youth facing charges of pot possession; of an over-weight minister who can't push away the rich dessert; of a candidate for the ministry who can't afford to stay in school because his cravings have depleted his resources.

The lives—and deaths of the rock stars are a collage of passion, violence, hedonism, exhaustion, and death. Janis Joplin stood for freedom. Her singing was unrestrained, filled with raw emotion. "I'd rather not sing than sing quiet," she said.

Offstage her actions matched her singing. Her appetites were unchecked: alcohol, men, fast cars. "Whatever you need, get it now," she said. "The other way you end up old and who needs it?"

In October 1970, Janis Joplin "got it now"—at 27 years of age she died in a Los Angeles motel room littered with liquor bottles, dead of an overdose of heroin! Janis' freedom was a freedom to die, not to live.

The Demands of Obedience

Total Christianity speaks to our indulgent age be-cause it offers us liberation from our appetites. The life that a believer finds in Christ is marked by the dethroning of self-will and the elevating of God's will.

Playboy says: "If you can afford it, enjoy it."

The "free" thinker says: "If it's natural, it's right."

But Jesus says: "If any man will come after Me, let him deny himself and take up his cross daily" (Luke 9:23, KJV).

The encounter with God through faith in Jesus

Christ strikes at the center of our allegiances. The Bible makes it clear that we cannot accept the love of God and continue to live for ourselves. A real believer is one who does the will of God, because what a person obeys reveals what kind of person he is.

In our evangelical zeal to reach the greatest number with the least demand, we have often created the impression that free grace is nothing other than cheap faith.

We have learned that the Gospel is relevant to any culture, and we have apparently concluded that faith in Christ makes few, if any, demands upon our life-styles.

But listen to a few of Jesus' words:

If you love Me,
  you will do what I command (John 14:15).
Whoever has My commands and obeys them,
  he is the one who loves Me (John 14:21).
A time is coming
  when all who are in their graves will hear
    His voice and come out—
  those who *have done good* will rise to live
    (John 5:28-29).
If anyone loves Me,
  he will obey My teaching (John 14:23).
Not everyone who says to Me, "Lord, Lord," will
    enter the kingdom of heaven,
but only *he who does* the will of My Father who
    is in heaven (Matt. 7:21).

According to Jesus, then, whether or not we have truly met God in life-changing faith is revealed by whom we obey.

The Complements of Faith and Obedience

For generations now many evangelicals have thought of faith and obedience as opposites: Obeying God's law means salvation by works; trusting God's grace means salvation without works. This sort of thinking, however, makes sheer nonsense of every biblical reference to doing the will of God as prerequisite to entering the kingdom. If faith and obedience are not opposites, but complementary ways of looking at a Christian reality, then many of the details of the Gospel lead to life.

An Example

The story of the rich young ruler, recorded in Matthew 19:16-22, is a vivid example.

Now a man came up to Jesus and asked, "Teacher, what good thing must I do to get eternal life?"

"Why do you ask Me about what is good?" Jesus replied. "There is only One who is good. If you want to enter life, obey the commandments."

"Which ones?" the man inquired.

Jesus replied, "Do not murder, do not commit adultery, do not steal, do not give false testimony, honor your father and mother," and "love your neighbor as yourself."

"All these I have kept," the young man said. "What do I still lack?"

Jesus answered, "If you want to be perfect, go, sell your possessions and give to the poor, and you will have treasure in heaven. Then come, follow Me."

When the young man heard this, he went away sad, because he had great wealth.

Many evangelicals see Jesus' counsel to the young man to sell out as trading one legal righteousness for another. But if Jesus is teaching that the renunciation of self is only the other side of the reception of Christ—then the story presents a timeless truth: One cannot say Yes to God and eternal life without saying No to self.

Eternal life is not found in the wealth of the world. The story shows there is much to admire in this man. Matthew tells us that he was young (v. 20). Life lay before him. A bright future awaited him. He was also rich (v. 22). Perhaps he and others believed this indicated that God had blessed him. Jews, like Americans today, admired wealth and often took it as a token of God's favor.

But there is more. In his account of this conversation, Luke tells us that the young man was a ruler. He had unquestioned leadership ability—he was already recognized as a ruler among a people who admired and respected age.

This man was so outstanding that he could not be ignored. He must have been a striking individual, the kind of successful young man that mothers point to for their sons to model and their daughters to marry.

As Linus of *Peanuts* fame says, however, "There is no heavier burden than a great potential."

In spite of his success and cultural virtues, the young ruler's soul was empty. He was haunted by the questions: "Where is life? What is worth living for?"

So strongly did he feel this that he sought out the most popular religious teacher of the time—Jesus of Nazareth—for the answer.

Doesn't the life of this young man teach us that nature is no adequate preparation for grace? The best the world has to offer can never secure the benefits of grace—until the soul surrenders its sovereignty to God.

In early December 1976, University of Chicago professor Martin Marty, writer of a twice-monthly commentary on current religious events called *Context,* spoke of the recent visibility of evangelicals in American society. He granted that in 1976 evangelicals seized the spotlight from Catholics and ecumenical Protestants. But this new visibility, he stated, raises some disturbing questions. One of the most penetrating was this: Is evangelicalism going to forget about its roots in restraint or in discipleship? He asked this question after observing that almost every dimension of the sexual revolution has by now been accepted in pop evangelicalism—so long as it occurs within marriage. That will be a very frail boundary indeed, he said, as the years pass.

The Sacrifice of Obedience

Is anything to be given up for the sake of Christian devotion in tomorrow's evangelicalism? That question deserves an answer, but it should be answered only after we have heard the scriptural Word regarding obedience.

Eternal life is found in the commands of God. Jesus told the rich ruler, "If you want to enter life, obey the commandments" (Matt. 19:17). Jesus did not say *how* life is to be found in obedience to the law of God; He simply underscored the truth that it *is*.

The mere mention of "laws" or "commands" sets our teeth on edge. We rebel against them. That is one reason we resist this aspect of total Christianity. We want freedom, and we think freedom is found by removing all restraints. But the Bible teaches that freedom from law means enslavement to instincts. There is no slave like the man free to do as he pleases, because what he pleases is self-destructive.

A few years ago a California psychiatrist complained that four out of every 10 teenagers and young adults who visited his medical center had a psychological sickness that he could do nothing about. According to the *Los Angeles Times*, it was simply this: "Each of them demands that his world conform to his uncontrolled desires. Society has provided him with so many escape routes that he never has had to stand his ground against disappointment, postponement of pleasure, and the weight of responsibility—all forces that shape character."

The psychiatrist added that "if the personality disorder persists far into adulthood," there will be a "society of pleasure-driven people, hopelessly insecure and dependent."

The *Times* article concluded, "When you take the controls of constraint off a youngster, he never learns to slow down or control his drive to demand and do what he wants." Can there, after all, be a place for law? (Cited from *Eternity* Magazine, Nov. 1971, p. 13.)

A difficulty arises, however, when we consider that the rich ruler had tried to find eternal life by keeping God's commands and had failed. The problem, then, is: How shall we regard the commands of God? Are they a series of laws which must be obeyed in order to earn salvation? Or are they an expression of the will of God who loves us unconditionally?

Jesus tried to show the rich ruler that *who* gives the commands is as important as *what* He commands. He wanted the young man to consider his personal relationship to Him. "Why do you ask *Me* about what is good?" (v. 17) Jesus emphasized the "Me" in order to stimulate the young man's thinking: "Who is this Man? Is He a teacher, a miracle worker, or is He something more?"

God's Law will always strike us as unnecessary weight in our attempts to soar in the air of personal freedom—until we see that His Law may be a love letter explaining that we are not equipped with wings. Happiness can only be ours when we give up our dreams of flying and learn to walk on earth with Jesus Christ.

When we learn from the Law who we are and who God is, it is possible to say with David and with Jesus: "O how I love Thy law" (Ps. 119:97).

Perhaps we can make the point by this story. A young man patronizes Burger King 192 times. He likes his hamburger with a big slice of onion. He never thinks of hamburgers without big slices of onions.

But one day he falls for a cute brunette on campus. He takes her to a football game and afterward they head for Burger King.

As he walks toward the counter he instinctively turns to Sue and says, "Do you like yours with or without?"

"Why, without, of course."

"Two without," he says.

Life has changed! Here is the explosive power of a new affection. The law of love has become the fount of life.

That is how God designed us. But with the young ruler it didn't happen.

Eternal life is found only in renouncing self and receiving Jesus. "If you want to be perfect," Jesus said, "go, sell your possessions and give to the poor, and you will have treasure in heaven. Then come, follow Me" (v. 21).

Jesus' attempts to get this young man to realize to whom he was talking do not suggest that eternal life can be earned by acts of kindness. There is no basis here for arguing that poverty itself leads to spiritual life, because Jesus was not giving advice to everyone. He was, rather, urging this young ruler to make a direct assault on his own covetousness, the one thing keeping him from eternal life. Self for this young man was wrapped up in money, so Jesus said, "Sell out!"

Our "thing" may or may not be money. But the truth is the same. *There is no receiving Christ without the renouncing of self.* Christ cannot rule in a life where pride is supreme. No man can serve two masters. Or to make the same point in other terms: *There is no faith in Christ without the repentance for sin.*

Repentance is not a once-for-all experience—as though we can get it over in a moment—it is a mark of Christian reality continually.

The Fruit of Our Salvation

The faith that ushers us into Christian reality is not an idea that we accept; it is a life we begin to live. That is why Jesus mentioned selling out and giving to the poor. While good works are not the *root* of our salvation, they are the *fruit* of it. They are evidence of it.

We are saved by faith alone but the faith that saves us is never alone. It leads to a new kind of behavior.

Martin Luther saw the depths of the relation between faith and obedience as few other men. In his book *On the Freedom of the Christian Man,* written in 1520, Luther explained,

The soul which with a firm faith cleaves to the promises of God is united with them, absorbed by them, penetrated, saturated, inebriated by their power. . . . No good work can be within the soul, but the Word and faith reign there. . . . Plainly then faith is enough for the Christian man. He has no need for works to be made just. . . . But he is not therefore to be lazy or loose. Good works do not make a man good, but a good man does good works. A bishop is not a bishop because he consecrates a church, but he consecrates a church because he is a bishop. . . . Thus we see that the Christian man lives not to himself but to Christ and his neighbor through love.

Total Christianity, then, means a changed life because faith strikes at self-centeredness, and places Christ at the center of life.

Dr. Donald Grey Barnhouse gave a striking illustration of this.

I live in the country. A few years ago a friend who raises strawberry plants by the tens of thousands told me that he had some plants left over at the end of the season and that he would send me some. The shipment arrived, and there were a thousand plants. The farmer who was working the land on shares put them in, and I looked forward to the strawberry season with great joy.

Along about the end of May or the beginning of June, I looked at the patch with delight. There were several thousand blossoms and my mouth watered with anticipation. The next day, about noon, I asked the farmer what he had been doing that morning, and he replied, "I have been picking the blossoms off the strawberry plants." I could hardly believe my ears. He then explained: "If you have strawberries the first year, the strength goes into the berries, and the plants become weak and will never produce very much in the future. But if you let the strength go into the plants the first year, you will have magnificent berries for years to come." And so it proved in the following years (*Eternity*, April, 1956).

In terms of total Christianity, then, there is a place for repentance, for restraint, for law. In the depths of our souls faith requires, in the words of Browning, both the plunge of the beggar and the rising of the prince.

Are there not, Festus, are there
  not, dear Michal,
Two points in the adventure of
  the diver,
One—when, a beggar, he
  prepares to plunge,
One—when, a prince, he rises
  with his pearl?
                    —Robert Browning,
                    "Paracelsus," Part 1

3

Truth:

The Mark of
Christian Theology

Some years ago I read in the *Christian Heritage* magazine a few lines that speak to a current need in Christian circles:

From the cowardice that dares not face new truth, the laziness contented with half-truth and the arrogance that thinks it knows all truths, Good Lord, deliver us.

In our conflict with the evil one we face no greater struggle today than the struggle to sort out rumors, slogans, half-truths, myths, flattery, and facts.

In C. S. Lewis' *The Screwtape Letters* (Macmillan, 1961), Screwtape's first letter to Wormwood advises him on how to negate the work of the Enemy in the soul of the Convert. "Jargon, not argument, is your best ally in keeping him from the Church. . . . Give him a grand general idea that he knows it all and that everything he happens to have picked up in casual talk and reading is 'the result of modern investigation'" (pp. 8, 10).

The devil's work is made easy by our current mood. A deep distrust of the rational grows and grows in our society. Medical experts can't agree on the need for mass immunization programs. The Federal Drug Administration can't determine which drugs are safe. Economists sharply disagree over what it will take to get the economy moving.

Whatever happened to the absolutes of scientific fact? We like to think of ourselves as hardheaded realists but we are fast becoming a bewildered and bamboozled generation. From every side some voice is screaming, pleading, or cajoling us to buy this or ban that.

So-called truth has been reduced to bumper sticker slogans. They must be brief, arresting, and cute. For example, "Legalize bingo. Get Grandma off the streets."

Behind the bumper sticker mentality is the assumption that conduct is a matter of mass appeal. Truth is in the greatest numbers. The absolute standard has become public opinion.

Charles Malik, former president of the United Nations General Assembly, identified the problem a number of years ago in his book *Christ and Crisis* (Eerdmans, 1962, p. 89). "Nothing," he said, "is more heroic today . . . than the spiritual struggle against the deception of words and the distortion of meanings and the bondage of cliches."

Today, as never before, we need to subject testimonies to rigid and searching inquiry. In our anti-intellectual generation, Christians, who follow the One who claimed to be the Truth, need:

to read,
to think,
to question,
to search,
to challenge.

There is a ministry today in helping people think straight. So many people approach Christianity with the expectation that the God who revealed Himself in Christ must be active today in some dramatic, emotion-stirring way!

We cannot effectively respond to these demands by treating the Living God as a retired Superstar of past generations. The Bible tells of a God who acts and speaks, and the testimony of Christian believers over the centuries is of God's unexpected power in their lives. The centuries have also shown that unchallenged rationalism is no friend of revealed religion. We may recall that the rationalists rejected a supernatural Jesus and assaulted an inspired Bible.

These facts make a balanced response to the current wave of emotionalism a top-drawer priority. Perhaps Blaise Pascal, the 17th century genius, assessed our problem best when he wrote: "If we submit everything to reason, our religion will have no mysterious and supernatural element. If we offend the principles of reason, our religion will be absurd and ridiculous."

While the Christian faith is more than how a man thinks, it is not less than that. We cannot surrender our faith to the forces of superstition or high feelings and think that we have Christianity. That is why fundamentalists, who poke fun at other conservatives who take their Christian scholarship seriously, are playing a deadly game.

The Gospel about Jesus Christ is Good News about facts. True Christian commitment, then, is based on truth. In this sense, Christianity is a rational religion. It challenges the mind, as well as the heart and the will, and every Christian should be clear as to what he believes and why he believes it.

Jesus showed this in His own ministry and teaching. Consider this passage:

One of the teachers of the Law came and heard them debating. Noticing that Jesus had given them a good answer, he asked Him, "Of all the commandments, which is the most important?"

"The most important one," answered Jesus, "is this: 'Hear, O Israel, the Lord our God, the Lord is one; love the Lord your God with all your heart, with all your soul, with all your mind and with all your strength.' The second is this: 'Love your neighbor as yourself.' There is no greater commandment than these."

"Well said, teacher," the man replied. "You are right in saying that God is one and there is no other but Him. To love Him with all your heart, with all your understanding and with all your strength, and to love your neighbor as yourself is more important than all burnt offerings and sacrifices."

When Jesus saw that he had answered wisely, He said to Him, "You are not far from the kingdom of God." And from then on no one dared ask Him any more questions (Mark 12:28-34).

The Mind in Ministry

Notice that Jesus employed the intellect in His ministry. "One of the teachers of the law came and heard them debating" (Mark 12:28).

Jesus' message was under attack from the Sadducees. They didn't believe in the resurrection (v. 18) and tried to show how ridiculous such a belief was. Jesus, however, argued from Scripture and quoted God's words to Moses: "I *am* the God of Abraham, and Isaac and Jacob" (Ex. 3:6)— showing in this way that He is Lord of the living.

It was clear that the Sadducees knew neither Scripture nor the power of God (v. 24). Jesus had the conviction and the courage to say they were wrong. He didn't accept their unbelief as just "their thing."

Today, many Christians try to make experience the primary standard of truth. What matters in the end, they say, is "not doctrine but experience."

Thank God for zeal. Heaven forbid that knowledge without zeal should replace zeal without knowledge! God's plan for His people is both— zeal directed by knowledge and knowledge fired by zeal.

God made man in His own image, and one of the noblest features of the divine likeness in man is his capacity to think. It is the prerequisite for receiving God's Word to man.

The Bible teaches that God has spoken. He has communicated in words. If nature is God's revelation visualized, then Scripture is God's revelation verbalized and Christ—"the Word made flesh" is both.

Our duty, then, is to receive God's message, to submit to it, to seek to understand it, and to relate it to the world in which we live.

The Mind in Worship
Notice also that Jesus commends the mind in worship. "Love the Lord your God with all your mind" (Mark 12:30).

When Jesus enters a person's life by faith, He enters as *Lord*. No area of life remains our own. Our minds, therefore, belong to Him, just as our time and our money belong to Him. Our intellect is no longer sovereign; it is in God's service.

Throughout the New Testament the worship of God "in truth" (John 4:24) remains the standard for Christians. Mindless worship to an "unknown God" (Acts 17:23) was characteristic of pagan worship at Athens, not of early Christian devotion.

Years ago the *British Weekly* (February, 1951) printed a little poem that expresses an all-too-common Christian condition:

I'm a Christian in my way.
How, it's difficult to say.
I've the haziest sort of notion
What I mean by my devotion.

Clichés clutter up my head,
Catchwords are my daily bread.
Exquisitely undefined
Is the thing I call my mind.

Peanuts character Linus said, "I love nature—people, birds, fish, plant life. I love without reservation. I love without thinking."

Many Christians live schizophrenic lives, loving God with their emotions and living in the world with their minds. But God has called us to wholeness—loving God with heart *and* mind.

John Baillie was a Scottish theologian who died in the early 1960s. In one of the books released after his death there is a biographical note about three objects in his study that are symbolic of the wholeness of his career. One was a desk where he wrote, the second was the chair where he read, and the third was the pad where he knelt daily to pray.

When I read that I thought of Paul's closing words to Timothy. "When you come bring the cloak that I left with Carpus at Troas and my scrolls, especially the parchments" (2 Tim. 4:13).

What have you read in the last month? How are you growing in your knowledge of our Lord Jesus?

The Mind in Evangelism
Finally, Jesus observed the mind in evangelism. The way we think can bring us near to the kingdom. When Jesus saw that the scribe answered wisely, He said to him, "You are not far from the kingdom of God" (Mark 12:34).

Paul summed up his evangelistic ministry in the simple words "we try to persuade men" (2 Cor. 5:11, NASB). Persuading, of course, is an intellectual exercise. It is marshalling arguments in order to prevail on people to change their minds.

Our duty as Christians is to avoid distorting or diluting the Gospel. At the same time we are to make it plain, to cut the Word of truth straight so that people can follow it (2 Tim. 2:15), lest "when anyone hears the message about the kingdom, and does not understand it, the evil one comes and snatches away what was sown in his heart" (Matt. 13:19). I fear that our clumsy explanations sometimes give the devil this very opportunity.

The Mind and the Holy Spirit

Jesus, of course, did not say that only proper *thinking* will make a person a disciple. There can be no evangelism without the power of the Holy Spirit. But Jesus did indicate that right thinking about the truth of God can bring a person to the point of faith and the regenerating witness of the Spirit. The beginning of faith is always repentance —a change of mind.

Perhaps the best example of the importance of right thinking about God's truth and our soul's need is in Martin Luther's struggle of soul with a fundamental *idea:* How does a man get right with God?

Born in 1483, the son of a Saxon miner, Luther had every intention of becoming a lawyer until, one day in 1505, he was caught in a sudden storm while walking toward the village of Stotternheim. A bolt of lightning knocked him to the ground, and Luther, terrified, called out to the church's patroness of miners: "Saint Anne, help me! I will become a monk!"

To his parents' dismay, Luther kept the vow.

Two weeks later he entered the Augustinian priory at Erfurt. And what a pious monk he was! "I kept the rule so strictly," he recalled years later, "that I may say that if ever a monk got to heaven by his sheer monkery it was I. If I had kept on any longer, I should have killed myself with vigils, prayers, reading, and other work."

What drove Luther to health-cracking rigors of austerity—he sometimes fasted for three days, slept without a blanket in freezing winter—was a profound sense of his own sinfulness and of God's unutterable majesty. Luther wrote that in the midst of saying his first mass, "I was utterly stupified and terror-stricken. I thought to myself, 'Who am I that I should lift up mine eyes or raise my hands to the divine majesty? For I am dust and ashes and full of sin, and I am speaking to the living, eternal and true God.'" No amount of penance, no soothing advice from his superiors could still Luther's conviction that he was a miserable, doomed sinner. Although his confessor counseled him to love God, Luther one day burst out, "I do not love God! I hate Him!"

Luther found that missing love in the study of Scripture. Assigned to the chair of biblical studies at Wittenburg University, he became fascinated and puzzled by the emphasis on righteousness in the Psalms and in Paul's epistles—notably in Romans 1:17 (KJV): "For therein is the righteousness of God revealed from faith to faith: as it is written, 'The just shall live by faith.'" As Luther later explained: "Night and day I pondered, until I saw the connection between the justice of God and the statement that 'the just shall live by faith.' Then I grasped that the justice of God is that righteousness by which, through grace and sheer mercy, God justifies us through faith. Thereupon I felt myself to be reborn and to have gone through open doors into paradise."

What a man believes *does make a difference.* This view—which we now call justification by faith alone—became the cornerstone of the Reformation. It ran strongly counter to medieval Catholic teaching which overemphasized the belief that man had to participate in, even earn, his salvation, and the forgiveness of temporal punishment for sin, by good works.

But for someone today who is ridden with guilt, anxiety, and fear—who is into his problems over his head—this comes as a liberating word: "God loves you. Christ died to free you. There is new life if you completely trust Him."

That is truth.

4

Conversion:

The Mark of Christian Experience

"God worked His way into my heart and changed my life." That is how country music singer Jeanne C. Riley explains her conversion. The pretty, blue-eyed brunette had gained fame as the seemingly brash, hip, and uninhibited young woman who ripped into her community's hypocrisy in her hit song, "Harper Valley PTA."

But it made her a rag-doll phony. "The world put me into the role of a sassy, show-off sex symbol. It was an image created for me and I hated it, but for a long time I couldn't step out of it, I was so stereotyped.

"I was playing a part that was not really me."

During that period, she said, she had "quit the church, doubted God's existence, and thought the Bible was just a big, beautiful myth. I simply had never thought much about spiritual things."

Then one hot afternoon in New Hope Cemetery,

she prayed alone at the new grave of a young nephew, Bryan, who had died at age six. "Oh God, I don't know if You're real," she had prayed, gazing up into the empty sky. "I've got to know, I've got to have a sign that You care." It was 3:45 P.M., she related, but suddenly, incredibly, in the bright, cloudless summer sky, "a giant star came out and held and twinkled for about 15 seconds."

As she told of it, her voice broke and tears streamed down her cheeks.

"There was no mistaking it, no way to doubt. I said, 'Oh, hello, Bryan!' And then the star came back and twinkled again. I cried, 'Thank You, God!' He had let me know He did exist, and I found Him later on in the Bible."

Miss Riley is an example of hundreds of public figures who have testified of their conversion experiences in recent years: Charles Colson, Jeb Stuart McGruder, Johnny Cash, Eldridge Cleaver.

The list reaches from Manson Family prison cells to Super Bowl starting line-ups to White House aides. Religious experiences are in.

Recently the *New York Times Magazine* reported the disturbing results of a survey. Andrew M. Greeley, well-known Catholic sociologist, and William C. McReady asked 1,500 people: "Have you ever had the feeling of being very close to a powerful spiritual force that seemed to lift you out of yourself?" They found that about 600 persons—two fifths of the 1,500 persons asked the question—reported having had at least one such experience. About 300 said they had had it several times, and 75 said they had had it often.

In a day when experiences are "in," we are forced to ask for ourselves and our ministries, "What experience?" What are the marks of a genuinely Christian conversion? How do you tell sterling from silverplate?

A person's direct experience with God has always been at the heart of evangelical Christianity. All the other aspects of "total Christianity"—Christian ethics, Christian theology, and Christian community —are shaped, evangelicals insist, by a person-to-person relationship with God.

Obviously, many experiences offered today are in sharp conflict with this one. Why do evangelical Christians insist that this meeting with God is the only true experience, the only life-fulfilling one? Because this life-changing meeting with God is what Jesus Christ provided through His sacrificial death and His resurrection.

The four Gospels are filled with person-to-person experiences, but the elements of a truly "evangelical" experience are probably seen best in John 4, which describes Jesus' meeting with a Samaritan woman.

When a Samaritan woman came to draw water, Jesus said to her, "Will you give Me a drink?" (His disciples had gone into the town to buy food.)

The Samaritan woman said to Him, "You are a Jew and I am a Samaritan woman. How can You ask me for a drink?" (For Jews do not associate with Samaritans.)

Jesus answered her, "If you knew the gift of God and who it is that asks you for a drink, you would have asked Him and He would have given you living water."

"Sir," the woman said, "You have nothing to draw with and the well is deep. Where can You get this living water? Are You greater than our father Jacob, who gave us the well and drank from it himself, as did also his sons and his flocks and herds?"

Jesus answered, "Everyone who drinks this water will be thirsty again, but whoever drinks the water I give him will never thirst. Indeed, the water I give him will become in him a spring of water welling up to everlasting life."

The woman said to Him, "Sir, give me this water so that I won't get thirsty and have to keep coming here to draw water."

He told her, "Go, call your husband and come back."

"I have no husband," she replied.

Jesus said to her, "You are right when you say you have no husband. The fact is, you have had five husbands, and the man you now have is not your husband. What you have just said is quite true."

"Sir," the woman said, "I can see that You are a prophet. Our fathers worshiped on this mountain, but you Jews claim that the place where we must worship is in Jerusalem."

Jesus declared, "Believe Me, woman, a time is coming when you will worship the Father neither on this mountain nor in Jerusalem. You Samaritans worship what you do not know; we worship what we do know, for salvation is from the Jews.

Yet a time is coming and has now come when the true worshipers will worship the Father in spirit and truth, for they are the kind of worshipers the Father seeks. God is spirit, and His worshipers must worship in spirit and in truth."

The woman said, "I know that Messiah" (called Christ) "is coming. When He comes, He will explain everything to us." Then Jesus declared, "I who speak to you am He."

Just then His disciples returned and were surprised to find Him talking with a woman. But no one asked, "What do You want?" or "Why are You talking with her?"

Then, leaving her water jar, the woman went back to the town and said to the people, "Come, see a man who told me everything I ever did. Could this be the Christ?" They came out of the town and made their way toward Him (vv. 7-30).

The Initiation of Experience (v. 7)

The first noteworthy element in this story is that Jesus opens the conversation. And that is basic to every truly Christian experience. God initiates the relationship. Saving faith must be seen as our human response to what God has already done and said, for throughout its pages the Bible portrays God as aggressively seeking men. How beautifully this is shown in Genesis! Adam disobeyed God. He sinned against God by seizing the forbidden fruit and fleeing from the presence of God. Who, then, reopened the conversation? It was God who came in the evening calling, "Adam, where are you?" (Gen. 3:9)

The God of the Bible assumes the responsibility for restoring the broken relationship with rebellious men. That is the point Jesus would make with the woman. "The Father," He told her, "seeks true worshipers" (John 4:23). That, in fact, is the meaning of Jesus' whole life. He is God seeking true worshipers, stooping to the level of broken humanity, putting Himself in need of this needy sinner when He asked her for a drink.

Surely the God who comes looking for lonely, estranged people is unique in the annals of world religions.

But that is a strange and foreign note in today's chorus of evangelical experiences. Evangelicalism is a movement that is supposed to celebrate the initiative and sovereignty of God—that is our Reformation and Puritan heritage—but we seem to be obsessed with power, personality, therapy, sensitivity, and human need. Where is God? Where is holiness? Where is theology?

The Barriers to Experience (vv. 9-26)

The Bible never allows Christian compassion to slide down into mere sentimentality, because the Bible isn't primarily concerned with human need. It is obsessed with the grace of God.

That is why this story about a much misused woman reveals the barriers the human heart can throw in the way of a life-changing encounter with God.

She thought the primary obstruction was a cultural barrier: "You are a Jew," she said, "and I am a Samaritan woman."

Ignorance of the grace of God. Jesus indicates that the first and primary barrier to meeting God is ignorance of His grace: "If you knew the gift of God" (v. 10).

Here is the birth of a missionary heart. It is not the compassion for the poor heathen in all their cultural trappings but the conviction that regardless of cultural differences the real need is grace, and therefore the real barrier to life with God is ignorance of the grace of God. "If you knew the gift of God."

But notice that this ignorance is not a matter of the mind; it is a matter of the heart. It wasn't some information she was lacking; it was what Jonathan Edwards called "religious affections." She could not know the gift of God until she had sensed her rebellion, so Jesus said, "Go, call your husband." That was devastating because she had had five husbands and was living with still another man at that moment.

In our day we wonder why Jesus chose to embarrass her by raising the issue. Most evangelical "soul-winner" efforts today would have asked her to fill out a decision card as soon as she said, "Give me this water." And you can be sure that her testimony about the conveniences of the new life—no more trips to the well—would be in the next issue of the missionary magazine.

J. Gresham Machen once said, "A low view of Law leads to legalism in religion; a high view of Law makes a man a seeker after grace" (*Origin of St. Paul's Religion,* p. 179). He was right.

Unwillingness to Repent. Before a person can

find Christian reality, that life-changing relation with God, he must recognize his profound spiritual bankruptcy. He must see himself as a moral rebel against God. He must surrender all attempts at self-justification. In this sense, it is not our sin that keeps us from God. It is our unwillingness to say, "I've failed and I'm sorry."

The woman was unwilling at first to face up to her spiritual poverty. She refused to accept her sin as the real barrier to fellowship with God. Rather than assume responsibility for her moral sickness, she tried to hide behind religious talk.

First, she raised a question about religious ritual. "Our fathers," she said, "worshiped on this mountain; and you say that in Jerusalem is the place where men ought to worship." That wasn't the last time a troubled soul sought to avoid moral responsibility by raising a point of discussion about some religious ceremony.

Jesus, however, told the woman that true worship consisted of meeting God not in special religious places but in spirit and in truth. He brought her again to the need of her own heart.

And she got the point because she again retreated, this time hiding behind theological talk. "I know that Messiah is coming," she said, "when He comes, He will explain everything to us" (John 4:25). She tried to substitute talk about God for a genuine encounter with God.

That is an ever present danger in evangelical churches, where open profession of faith "with the mouth" is highly valued or even required. Profession may easily be taken for conversion. Knowing the right words to use can easily be substituted for seeking a true experience of God's grace. This is often the "confessional fallacy" of some evangelicals.

John Wesley, who made a great contribution to the early evangelical revivals, is himself an example of the futility of offering religious rituals and theological talk as substitutes for the genuine experience of God's grace and peace.

Wesley was an ordained priest of the Church of England, a devout churchman, a brilliant scholar, and a man of high moral character. He believed the creed; he followed the commandments; he was full of good works. But he lacked peace and assurance that all was right between himself and God.

Fired by zeal for the service of God, he sailed for the British colony of Georgia to serve as chaplain to the governor of the colony and to engage in missionary service. There he met some humble Moravians. One of them, Pastor Spangenberg, pressed home to Wesley the challenging personal question, "Does the Spirit of God bear witness with your spirit that you are a child of God?"

Poor Wesley! Spangenberg, like Jesus long before him, had touched the raw nerve of spiritual need. Wesley had no spiritual assurance until later, back home in London, God moved in and he was profoundly converted. He met Jesus!

So did the Samaritan woman, there at the well. When her barriers crumbled, Jesus told her directly, "I who speak to you am Messiah." That moment all her defenses came down and in faith she accepted Jesus as her Messiah.

The Effect of Experience (vv. 27-30)

The account of the conversation nowhere says that the woman experienced the life of God, but the effects are clearly there. She immediately left her water jar and returned to the city. "Come," she cried, "see a man who told me all that I ever did. Can this be the Messiah?" (v. 29)

That says a great deal about the depth of her experience, because the essence of Christian experience is not monastic withdrawal or rapturous emotional highs. It is a spontaneous desire to share the joy of Christ and to bring others to Him.

John Bunyan presented this dramatic movement from conviction of sin to salvation in *The Pilgrim's Progress*. Weighted down by an overwhelming sense of sin—symbolized by a heavy burden on his back which he cannot unfetter—Christian comes, in the course of his journey, to a highway "fenced on either side with a Wall . . . called Salvation." Running upwards, "burdened Christian" reaches a place where "stood a Cross, and a little below in the bottom, a Sepulchre. So I saw in my dream," writes Bunyan,

> that just as Christian came up with the Cross, his burden loosed from off his shoulders, and fell from off his back, and began to tumble; and so continued to do, till it came to the mouth of the sepulchre, where it fell in, and I saw it no more.
>
> Then was Christian glad and lightsome, and said with a merry heart, "He hath given me rest, by His sorrow; and life, by His death."
>
> Then Christian gave three leaps for joy, and went on singing.

"Thus far did I come loaden with my sin,
Nor could ought ease the grief that I was in,
Till I came hither: . . .
Blest Cross! blest sepulchre!
Blest rather be
The Man that there was put to shame for me."

This experience of spiritual liberation and rapturous joy, arising from Jesus Christ personally received, constitutes the subjective center of total Christianity. In our day of countless experiences, this is the hallmark for distinguishing reality from fantasies.

5

Church:

The Mark of
Christian Community

The Bible speaks of heaven as a city; and it describes hell as solitary confinement. The reason may be that God designed man for community. It isn't good for man to be alone. That is why we can never talk about total Christianity without considering the church.

The word stirs bitter thoughts in the minds of some people because somewhere in their memories "church" meant boredom, bondage, or even rejection. A minister disappointed them or some congregation misled them. It isn't hard to find people who are "turned off" by church.

The Bible, however, teaches that God designed the church as the remedy for our self-centeredness, loneliness, and alienation. A *Peanuts* cartoon shows Lucy saying to Linus: "Charlie Brown says that we're put here on earth to make others happy." Replies Linus: "Is *that* why we're here? I guess I'd

better start doing a better job . . . I'd hate to be
shipped back!" If one of the reasons for our being
on earth is to make others happy, we need the
church. Why? Because the church was designed
to be a community of men and women freed from
themselves in order to seek the happiness of others.

Jesus Himself said very little about the church.
He preferred to teach the lessons of life in a spiritual fellowship by speaking about the kingdom.
By the kingdom Jesus usually meant the rule of
God in the hearts of men—as we discovered in our
study of the rich young ruler (Matt 19:23). On
another occasion, Jesus told Nicodemus that man
had to be born again to enter the kingdom of God
(John 3:3). We can only enter the kingdom, He
said, by saying a decisive no to ourselves—He
called this repentance. (The word means "a change
of mind," and the greatest change comes in no
longer feeding our pride, but saying "no" to our
self-will, and humbly believing that through Jesus
we are children of God.

This He called faith (Mark 1:15-18). His para-
bles are filled with people who sought or shunned
this kingdom (Matt. 22:1-14; 18:21-35).

Only twice did Jesus refer to the church. The
first occasion was a conversation at Caesarea
Philippi (Matt. 16:13-23; see also Matt. 18:15-20).
With His companions Jesus raised three issues:

Who is the Son of Man? (Matt. 16:13-16)

What is the church? (vv. 17-20)

Why the Cross? (vv. 21-23)

This is the way Matthew remembered it:

When Jesus came to the region of Caesarea

Philippi, He asked His disciples, "Who do people say the Son of Man is?"

They replied, "Some say John the Baptist; others say Elijah; and still others, Jeremiah or one of the prophets."

"But what about you?" He asked. "Who do you say I am?"

Simon Peter answered, "You are the Christ, the Son of the living God."

Jesus replied, "Blessed are you, Simon son of Jonah, for this was not revealed to you by man, but by My Father in heaven. And I tell you that you are Peter, and on this rock I will build My church, and the gates of Hades will not overcome it. I will give you the keys of the kingdom of heaven, and whatever you bind on earth will be bound in heaven, and whatever you loose on earth will be loosed in heaven." Then He warned His disciples not to tell anyone that He was the Christ.

From that time on Jesus began to explain to His disciples that He must go to Jerusalem and suffer many things at the hands of the elders, chief priests and teachers of the law, and that He must be killed and on the third day be raised to life.

Peter took Him aside and began to rebuke Him. "Perish the thought, Lord!" he said. "This shall never happen to You!"

Jesus turned and said to Peter, "Out of My sight, Satan! You are a stumbling block to Me; you do not have in mind the things of God, but the things of men" (16:13-23).

Here Jesus was teaching His disciples three fundamental lessons about the community He came to create.

A Confessing Community

First, the church is to be a community that knows who Jesus Christ is and teaches the truth about Him (Matt. 16:13-16). It is to "confess" or "acknowledge" Him.

The place Jesus chose to test His disciples' understanding of the truth added impact to His question: "Who do you say I am?" Near Caesarea Philippi rose a great hill and in it was a deep cavern which was said to be the birthplace of Pan, the Greek god of nature. Caesarea Philippi itself also boasted a great temple of white marble built by Herod the Great in honor of the godhead of Caesar.

To this place Jesus chose to take His disciples. And what a dramatic picture it must have presented: a homeless, penniless Galilean carpenter, asking 12 ordinary men about His deity!

It is as if Jesus deliberately set Himself against the background of Greek and Roman religion and forced His disciples to render their verdict on His Messiahship. Before He set out for Jerusalem and the cross, He had to know if they had grasped who He was and the significance of His mission.

Responsible Christian community begins there—at the point of truth regarding Jesus. These men would learn much more about the faith they were called to believe and preach, but their direction in that truth was set by this fundamental question: "Who do you say I am?"

Let this serve as a reminder to us that Christianity means community in and through Jesus Christ. We belong to one another only because we all belong to Him.

If someone asks, "Where is your salvation? Where is your righteousness?" a Christian can never point to himself. He can only point to the Word of God, which assures him of salvation in Jesus Christ. In himself, the believer is only destitute and dead, but in Christ he finds community and life.

Notice too how Jesus led the disciples in sorting out personal conviction from public opinion. "Who do people say the Son of Man is?"

They answered, "Some say John the Baptist, others say Elijah, and still others Jeremiah or one of the prophets."

In the history and tradition of Israel that was illustrious company! The public intended a high compliment when they associated Jesus with the prophets.

But Jesus moved these future leaders of the church beyond public opinion. "And how about you? Who do you say I am?"

Our knowledge of Jesus can never be second-hand. A person might be able to summarize the teachings of Jesus, supporting each point by chapter and verse, and still not be qualified for Christian community, because *knowing about Jesus* is not the same as *knowing Jesus*. Public opinion simply will not do. Christian community must spring from personal conviction.

The church today also has the responsibility of sorting out truth from public opinion. Our world is caught up in a war of words: twisted terms, half-truths, rhetoric, unfounded accusations, libel, labels, charges, and denials. Public relations experts, trained in skills of qualifications, empty generalities, and meaningless phrases, draw sizeable salaries not to establish the truth but to create public opinion. In this climate the Christian community must be able to distinguish clearly fact from fad.

Abraham Lincoln once asked a debate opponent: "If you call a dog's tail a leg—how many legs has a dog got?"

The opponent thought for a second and said: "Well, if you count the tail as a leg—I guess you would have to say he had five legs."

"That's where you're wrong," said Lincoln. "Even if you call a dog's tail a leg—it isn't one; it's still a tail."

Lincoln was right—calling a tail a leg doesn't make it one. Ten thousand people can call it a leg and it's still a tail.

The Christian community must beware of this demon of the popular. Satan knows most about "how to win friends and influence people." This is why so many Christians are tempted to listen to his advice and bow at the shrine of the public image. The great test of Christian community in our society is whether a man makes a decision that is popular or one that is right.

As we face the temptation to equate success with keeping the maximum number happy, is there any guideline to help us find out the way? Yes, it is the "truth as it is in Jesus": His incarnation, His life, His death, His resurrection, His salvation. Because Peter caught a glimpse of that and refused the enslavement of popular opinion, Jesus detected his leadership potential for the Christian community.

A Triumphant Community

After Peter's confession, Jesus shifts from questioning to stating: "I will build My church."

Matthew 16:17-20 has been a storm-center of controversy for centuries and it is almost impossible to approach this passage for growth of the faith rather than defense of the faith. But I'd like us to think of it in terms of the character of this fledgling community. What was Jesus trying to get across to Peter and the other Apostles?

This is probably Jesus' only discussion of the church. What would the Twelve need to know in order to assume leadership in the community in the coming months?

They would need to *identify the foundation of the church*. What are its basic realities? What is its inner genius?

Jesus identified the source of the church's life when He responded to Peter's confession: "This was revealed to you by God" (v. 17). In effect Jesus said to Peter: "Peter, you are the first man to grasp who I am and this revelation—this confession—which you made will be the foundation of the church of all true believers in Me."

We must never forget that the church stands for

light in darkness, for a sure word in an uncertain world, for truth in a cacophony of lies.

Samuel Beckett's play *Waiting for Godot* is a remarkable reflection of our modern mood. The play is simply a meandering conversation of two bums waiting for a Mr. Godot, who never comes.

Vladimir, one of the bums, finally says, "What are we doing here, that is the question. And we are blessed in this, that we happen to know the answer. Yes, in this immense confusion one thing alone is clear. We are waiting for Godot to come—or for night to fall."

Vladimir is surely a symbol of modern man. Must we continue to hover between a formless anticipation and the prospect of oblivion?

The Christian Gospel says No. God has come. He has broken the silence and in Jesus Christ He has spoken the good Word. There is not only Someone "out there" or "up there," but that Someone has communicated with us. In fact, He has told us that He loves us and has come to free us from our sin and senselessness.

Every Christian community must keep this fundamental concept in view. It is so easy to turn the church into a base for social change or social conservatism; into a cut-rate counseling center; or into a dozen other distortions of its true calling—a fellowship of men and women who have heard God's Word and now confess Jesus as Messiah, the Son of God.

To assume leadership in the Christian community, Peter and the other Apostles would also need to *rest in the victory of the church*. Jesus taught

these early leaders of the church that their cause—
a confessing fellowship in Christ—would prevail.
"The gates of Hades will not overcome it." What
a powerful way to assure the Apostles of the per-
petuity of the church!

Hades, in Jewish thinking, was the realm of the
dead. One purpose of gates is to keep things *in,*
but there was one person whom the gates of Hades
could not shut in. That was Jesus. He burst the
bonds of death. As Peter would announce in his
message at Pentecost: "God raised Him from the
dead . . . because it was impossible for death to
keep its hold on Him" (Acts 2:24).

The early Christians' faith, resting in the Risen
One, is the reason behind the rapid spread of Christianity throughout the Roman Empire and beyond
its borders. It is the explanation of the Christian
martyrs.

Some churches today seem less certain of their
mission in the world and more inclined to smile
upon life without God. We can trace this change
to a loss of faith in the One whom death could not
hold. More than mere doctrine must support true
Christian community—it must rest in a supernatural
Saviour. This is what Jesus was suggesting at
Caesarea Philippi. Victory for the church is guaran-
teed by the power of His resurrection.

What a resource for inspiring a following! Certain victory! People want to be identified with a
winner. Follow any high school, college, or pro
football team—and you will notice an interesting
characteristic of human nature: the winners draw
the crowds; losers play in half-empty stadiums.

Why? Because people want to be identified with victory.

In the Christian community we need the assurance that our "labors are not in vain." But for Bible-believing Christians, this is more than mental gymnastics. .It is response to God's certainties: the gates of hell shall not prevail!

A Selfless Community

Peter and the other Apostles had one more basic lesson to learn about spiritual community—the hardest lesson of all, the lesson of the *Cross* (Matt. 16:21-23).

Immediately after the exchange at Caesarea Philippi, Jesus began to tell His disciples that Jerusalem was His destination and that there He would be seized and killed. God's way led to Calvary.

But Peter said, "No!" He "caught hold" of Jesus. He flung a protecting arm around Jesus and said, "This must not and cannot happen to You!"

And then came Jesus' rebuke, "Get behind Me, Satan." Jesus heard in Peter's voice the accent of the tempter, who two or three years earlier had offered Him the kingdoms of the world—without the Cross. Peter had come far enough to confess Jesus but he had yet to learn that fundamental to Christian community is the crucifixion of self.

After 25 years in the Christian ministry one develops a few convictions. One of mine is that the greatest single hindrance to God's work in the world through His people in community is found in one three-letter word: ego. What untold damage has been done to Christian work and Christian churches by Christian people with the will to have their own way! Pastors who will not resign. Missionaries who never learned to serve. Members of congregations who never really join the church, but merely use it for a stage.

One simple test of our capacity for genuine Christian community can be measured by one simple question: What do we do with criticism?

It may help to recall a story about Samuel Johnson, the famous man of letters, who, almost single-handedly compiled the first "scholarly" dictionary of the English language. This book contained some mistakes, and occasionally these were brought to Johnson's attention in no flattering way.

On one occasion a pompous wealthy widow cornered him and in a rather malicious way asked how he could have defined *pastern* as the knee of a horse when it was obviously part of a horse's foot.

Taking a firm grip upon his mental faculties and looking the woman squarely in the eye, Johnson replied:

"Ignorance, madam; pure ignorance!"

I wonder how many of us have the courage to reply in such a forthright way when we are confronted by some error we have made in the work of God.

The church, however, is not a community of the perfect; it is a family of the forgiven. Nor is it, contrary to popular thought, made up of those who have arrived, but of those who are on the way.

If Jesus taught the disciples that true Christian community begins with the confession of Jesus as

Lord, He surely intended that it should be sustained by believers' confessions of faults. Someone has said: "The ego and the egg—both must be broken before they can be used." It is true in the kitchen and in the church.

"It is futile," Archbishop William Temple once said, "saying to people, 'Go to the Cross.' We must be able to say, 'Come to the Cross.' And there are only two voices which can issue that invitation with effect. One is the voice of the sinless Redeemer, with which we cannot speak; the other is the voice of the forgiven sinner, who knows himself forgiven. That is our part."

In his book, *Say It With Love*, (Victor Books, 1972) Howard Hendricks tells about a dream a man once had. In his dream, people were sitting along both sides of a sumptuous banquet table covered with delicious foods of every variety. But everyone had a baffling problem. Their arms were bound to boards and they could not bend their elbows. They managed to reach the food but could not get it in their mouths! Can you imagine anything more frustrating?

Finally one guest swung his arm to the fellow across the table and put his food in the other man's mouth. The second fellow returned the favor, and in no time everyone at the banquet was enjoying a delicious meal.

The dream demonstrates how Christian community is only possible when we are willing to admit our need of others.

We began this study of total Christianity with the conversation Jesus had with His disciples the night of His betrayal. We found that Peter, even at that late hour, thought of Christian *obedience* in terms of self-sacrifice rather than as the overflow of confidence in the Lord. We discovered that Thomas, just hours before the unique revelation of God in the Cross, doubted that life-changing *truth* could be found. We saw how Philip, after three years of travel with Jesus, still looked for some special *experience* that would disclose God to him, rather than resting in the depiction of God found in Jesus' life and witness. And, finally we heard Judas (or Thaddaeus) question the special character of Christian *community* which Jesus said was marked by love for Him.

If these men had trouble with total Christianity, it shouldn't surprise us when some Christians today claim that Christianity is a religious ethic, a doctrinal system, a high-powered experience, or a sacred institution. Total Christianity, in a word, is Christ. That is what He tried to get His first disciples to see. He was their Law, their Truth, their Life, their Oneness. And for us, that is still the crux of the matter.

ADULT ELECTIVE SHORT STUDIES

Six-session elective studies on short Bible books and current topics. Excellent for weekend retreats, home Bible studies, mid-week sessions, Vacation Bible School, Sunday School, as well as for personal study and spiritual growth.

CAN YOU RUN AWAY FROM GOD? James Montgomery Boice gives a very warm and human understanding of God's sovereignty versus man's free will in this study of the Book of Jonah. Textbook 6-2501—$1.50/Leader's Guide 6-2853—75¢

FOUND: GOD'S WILL (formerly *God's Will Is Not Lost*) John MacArthur, Jr. directs a very logical and biblical discussion on how to find God's will for your life. Textbook 6-2503—$1.25/Leader's Guide 6-2852—75¢

HOW TO GET UP WHEN YOU'RE DOWN Lowell Lundstrom, an evangelist, gives practical and biblical guidance on facing up to and overcoming discouragement. Textbook 6-2502—$1.25/Leader's Guide 6-2854—75¢

JOHN BUNYAN AND PILGRIM'S PROGRESS A devotional classic edited by Erwin P. Rudolph. Textbook 6-2505—$1.25/Leader's Guide 6-2856—75¢

LIGHT IN THE VALLEY Herbert Vander Lugt takes a practical, humane, and biblical approach in this short study on death and dying. Textbook 6-2504—$1.50/Leader's Guide 6-2851—75¢

RUN YOUR LIFE BY THE STARS? Edited by William J. Petersen, of *Eternity* magazine. A study that looks at astrology and what the Bible says about it. Textbook 6-2506—$1.25/Leader's Guide 6-2855—75¢

Add 40¢ postage and handling for the first book, and 10¢ for each additional title. Add $1 for minimum order service charge for orders less than $5.

**Buy these titles at your local
Christian bookstore or order from**

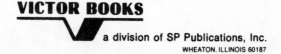

VICTOR BOOKS

a division of SP Publications, Inc.
WHEATON, ILLINOIS 60187